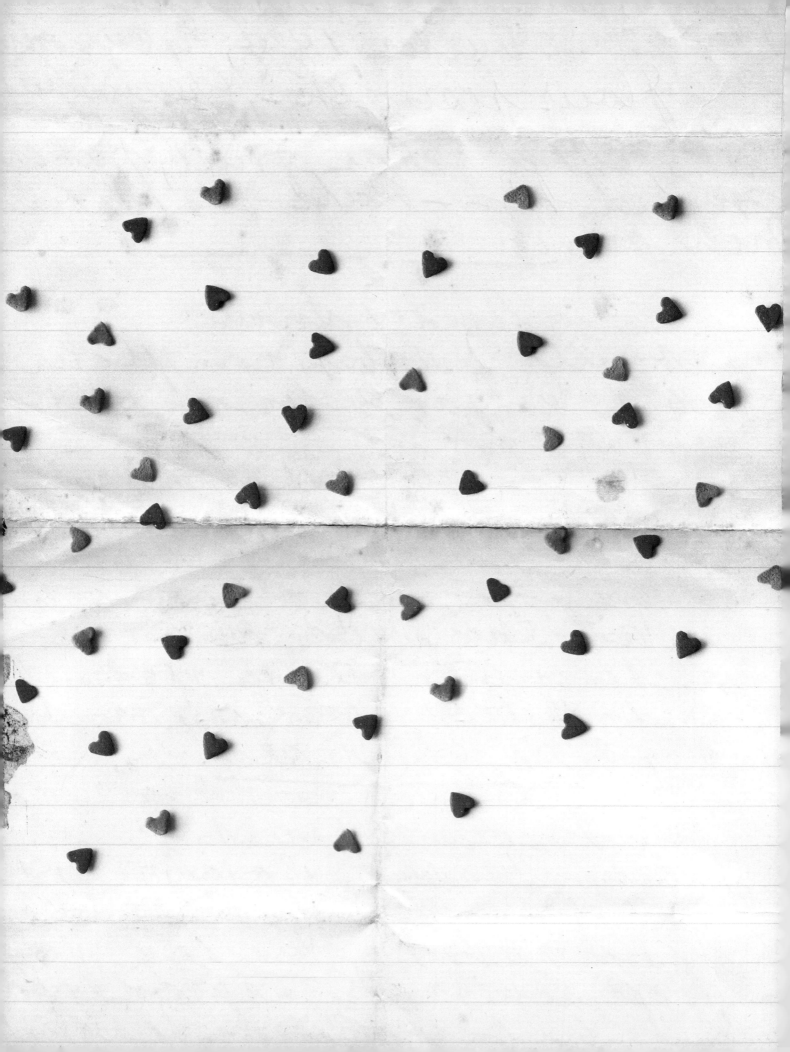

My Grandma's Kitchen

My Grandma's Kitchen

Louise Fulton Keats
recipes by Margaret Fulton
illustrations by Michelle Mackintosh

hardie grant books
MELBOURNE · LONDON

Contents

To my Grandma,
Margaret.
How lucky we all
are to have you.

My Grandma's kitchen is the best place to be!

We're ever so busy, Grandma and me.

We have all sorts of gadgets that go whizz and whir

And there's always a bowl Grandma needs me to stir.

Grandma loves when I help her – she has lots to do.

She's even made an apron with my name – 'Lulu'.

When I wear it I feel like a real, proper cook

With a chef's hat, a whisk and a recipe book.

Harry, my brother, also loves Grandma's kitchen.
Even though he's quite small, I let him join in.
I teach him to dice and to chop up a lettuce –
After all, a top chef like me needs an apprentice!

Breakfast

Eggs in ramekins

1 teaspoon olive oil

1 rasher free-range bacon,
   rind removed and diced

1 tablespoon finely chopped
   parsley or chives

1 spring onion, finely sliced

2 eggs

5 g butter

buttered toast fingers,
   to serve

Heat the oil in a small frying pan over medium heat and saute the bacon for a few minutes, or until golden brown.

Grease two small ramekins and divide the bacon, herbs and spring onion between them. Place the ramekins in a saucepan or deep frying pan and add enough water to reach halfway up the sides of the dishes. Crack an egg into each ramekin and top with a dot of butter. Cover and cook over low heat for 5–7 minutes, or until the eggs have set. Serve with buttered toast fingers.

Serves 2

I ask Grandma each morning, 'What are you making?'
She says, 'Eggs in ramekins with parsley and bacon.'
Of all Grandma's brekkies, I love this one the most
And it tastes even better with buttery toast!

Some mornings we have bircher muesli with yoghurt.

According to Grandma, we first need to soak it.

When it's ready to eat we add strawberries and pear

And give Teddy two servings ... he's one hungry bear!

Apple bircher muesli

1 cup rolled oats
1 cup apple juice
1 apple, grated
⅓ cup natural or
   fruit yoghurt

6 strawberries, hulled
   and quartered
1 pear, cored and sliced
honey, to serve (optional)

Combine the oats and apple juice in a large bowl, cover with plastic wrap and place in the fridge for 1 hour (or even overnight), until the juice has mostly soaked in.

Stir the apple and yoghurt through the oats. Divide between 3 bowls and top with the strawberries, pear and, if you like, a drizzle of honey.

Serves 3

Fluffy omelette

3 eggs, separated
salt and freshly ground
  black pepper
2 teaspoons plain flour

½ cup milk
20 g butter
¼ cup grated cheddar
  cheese

Whisk the egg yolks with a pinch of salt and pepper and the flour, then beat in the milk. Using an electric mixer, beat the egg whites until they form soft peaks, then fold lightly into the yolk mixture.

Preheat the grill to medium–high. Melt the butter in a non-stick frying pan, pour in the mixture and cook over low heat until set and golden underneath. Sprinkle the cheese on top then brown under the grill for 2–4 minutes (the omelette will puff up under the grill, but will sink back down again when removed). If you like, top the omelette with a filling such as herbs, cooked mushrooms or cooked tomatoes, then fold in half and serve.

Serves 2

Grandma also cooks omelettes – they're yummy for brekky.
I ask, 'How can you possibly make them so fluffy?'
She says, 'My little trick is to beat the egg white.'
We make a big one to share – but I get first bite!

Croque monsieur

butter
4 slices wholemeal
    bread

4 slices free-range
    leg ham
4 slices gruyere or
    emmenthal cheese

Preheat a sandwich press. Spread some butter on each slice of bread (the buttered side goes on the outside of the sandwich). Divide the ham between two slices of bread, then top with the cheese and another slice of bread. Cook in the sandwich press for 2–3 minutes, or until they are golden brown and the cheese has melted. If you don't have a sandwich press, you can cook the sandwiches in a frying pan over medium heat with a knob of butter. Cut into triangles or halves to serve.

Makes 2 sandwiches

The French usually make croque monsieur with white bread, but we like to use wholemeal, which is healthier and just as delicious!

I also love Grandma's grilled sandwiches with cheese.

They're delicious with ham – Harry agrees.

Grandma lets me eat them sitting up on her bench

And she tells me they're called 'croque monsieur' in French.

Grandma makes the best ever smoothies with peaches.
'Harry, we could make these! Let's ask Grandma to teach us!'
Pretty soon, thanks to Grandma, I'm a smoothie expert.
All you need is a blender, some milk and yoghurt!

Peach smoothie

400 g plastic tub peach slices, drained (or 2 peaches, peeled and chopped)

¼ cup natural yoghurt

1 cup milk
1 tablespoon honey
1 tablespoon wheatgerm (optional)
4 ice cubes

Place all the ingredients in a blender and process until smooth and frothy.

Serves 2

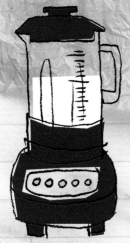

Crepes

1¼ cups plain flour

3 eggs

1½ cups milk

10 g butter, melted

extra butter, for frying

caster sugar and lemon
wedges, to serve

Sift the flour into a bowl. Make a well in the centre and add the eggs and milk. Start whisking the wet ingredients, gradually drawing in the flour. Stir in the melted butter and transfer the batter to a jug. If you have time, let the mixture stand (an hour or two is great, or even overnight).

Melt a little butter in a non-stick frying pan over medium heat. When the butter is bubbling, pour in enough batter to cover the bottom of the pan and swirl to spread evenly. Cook the crepes for about 1 minute each side, or until golden. Serve hot, sprinkled with sugar and a squeeze of lemon juice.

Makes about 12

You can make paper-thin crepes or thicker pancakes, depending on how much batter you add to the pan. Why don't you try both and see which one you like best?

On a Saturday morning Grandma makes us some crepes.

She makes big ones and small ones in all different shapes.

When we sprinkle the sugar, 'No snowfields!' she calls out,

But if we're quick with the lemon, she never finds out!

Pikelets

1 cup self-raising flour
2 tablespoons sugar
1 egg
1 cup milk (or ½ cup milk
    and ½ cup buttermilk)

40 g butter, melted
extra butter, for frying and
    to serve
jam, to serve

Sift the flour and sugar into a bowl. Make a well in the centre and add the egg, milk and melted butter. Start stirring the wet ingredients, gradually drawing in the dry ingredients. Stir until just combined. Do not overmix – it should be slightly lumpy.

Melt a little butter in a non-stick frying pan over medium heat. When the butter is bubbling, drop large spoonfuls of the batter into the pan and cook for 1 minute, or until bubbles appear on the surface. Turn and cook on the other side until golden. Repeat with the remaining mixture. Serve the pikelets warm or cool with butter and jam.

Makes about 15

You can make berry pikelets by lightly stirring ½ cup of fresh or frozen blueberries or raspberries through the batter.

On Sundays we always cook pikelets together.

Grandma knows how to make them as light as a feather.

We each take a turn flipping them in the pan,

Then we pile them up high with Grandma's strawberry jam.

Quick strawberry jam

500 g strawberries,
washed and hulled

¼ cup lemon juice
1½ cups sugar

Put the strawberries and lemon juice in a large
microwave-proof bowl. Cook on high, uncovered,
for 3 minutes. Add the sugar, stir well and cook
on high for a further 20 minutes, or until the jam
thickens a little. Allow to cool for about 5 minutes,
then stir to make sure the sugar is fully dissolved.
Ladle into sterilised jars and seal.
Makes about 2 cups

Grandma has a big garden with herbs by the bunch.

We pick lots of basil to use in our lunch.

It goes whizz in the blender and in minutes – hey presto!

We've made a big bowl of delicious green pesto.

Penne with pesto

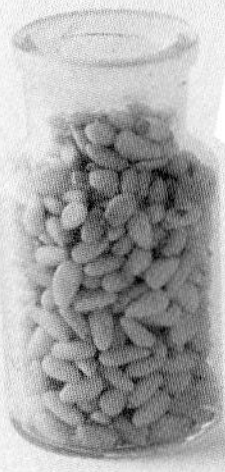

1½ cups firmly packed
   basil leaves

2 tablespoons pine nuts or
   chopped walnuts

½ cup grated parmesan
   cheese

2 cloves garlic, chopped

½ cup olive oil

500 g penne

30 g butter

extra parmesan
   cheese, to serve

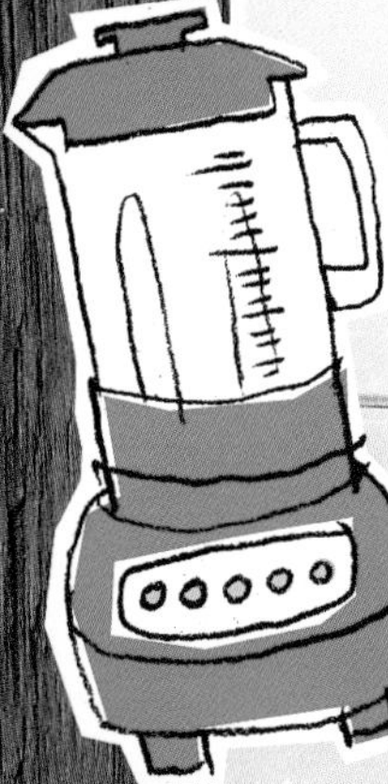

In a food processor, blend the basil, nuts, cheese and garlic, scraping down the sides occasionally, until almost smooth. Add the oil in a slow, thin stream and blend until smooth.

Cook the penne according to the instructions on the packet. Drain and return to the pan. Add the pesto and butter and toss over gentle heat for 2 minutes. Serve with extra parmesan cheese on top.

Serves 4–6

Herby potato salad

2 eggs

4 medium-large potatoes (desiree or similar variety)

salt and freshly ground black pepper

1½ tablespoons white balsamic or white wine vinegar

2 tablespoons extra-virgin olive oil

2 tablespoons finely chopped parsley

2 tablespoons finely snipped chives

2 spring onions, finely sliced

1 celery stalk, finely sliced

⅓ cup mayonnaise

Hard-boil the eggs (this will take about 10 minutes) and set aside to cool.

Boil the potatoes until tender and allow to cool before peeling the skin off with your fingers. Cut each potato into 8 pieces, place in a large bowl and season with salt and pepper to taste. Add the vinegar, oil, herbs, spring onion and celery and mix well. Leave for a few minutes to allow the dressing to absorb.

Peel and quarter the eggs. Add to the bowl with the mayonnaise and gently toss. Serve at room temperature.

Serves 4–6

Out in the garden I also pick parsley.

Harry, my trusty assistant, helps me.

How should we cook it? Grandma always knows ...

'Lulu, parsley is perfect tossed through potatoes!'

Minestrone

1 tablespoon olive oil

4 rashers free-range bacon,
   rind removed and diced

2 cloves garlic, finely chopped

1 brown onion, finely chopped

1 large carrot, diced

2 celery stalks, diced

2 tablespoons tomato paste

2 large tomatoes, diced

5 cups beef or vegetable stock

¾ cup small pasta shells or
   macaroni

1 cup fresh or frozen peas

1 zucchini (courgette), diced

150 g green beans, trimmed and
   cut into short lengths

400 g can cannellini beans,
   drained and rinsed

½ cup chopped parsley

salt and freshly ground black
   pepper

grated parmesan cheese,
   to serve

Heat the oil in a large saucepan and saute the bacon, garlic, onion,
carrot and celery for 4–5 minutes, or until the onion is tender. Add
the tomato paste and tomatoes and saute for a further minute. Add
the stock and 2 cups of cold water. Bring to the boil then reduce
the heat and simmer, covered, for 40 minutes. Add the pasta, peas,
zucchini, green beans and cannellini beans and simmer, covered,
for a further 15 minutes, or until the pasta is tender. Stir in the
parsley and season with salt and pepper to taste. Serve
topped with parmesan cheese.

Serves 4–6

Next to the herbs we grow beans and zucchini.

We pick them and chop them to make minestrone.

I tell Harry, 'You get to stir in the pasta and peas ...

'And I'll be in charge of the parmesan cheese!'

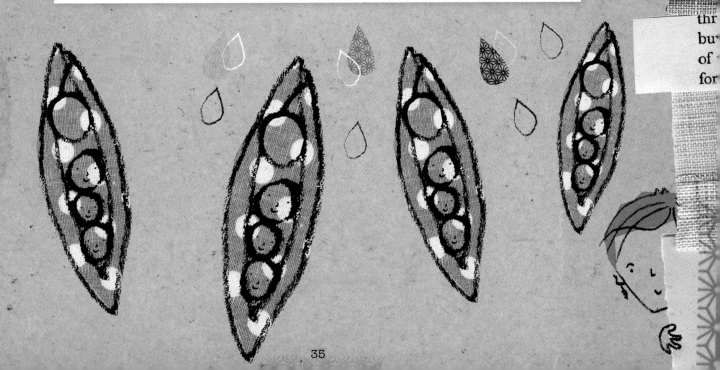

thr
bu
of
for

Margherita pizza

2 cups plain flour
1 teaspoon salt
1 teaspoon sugar
7 g sachet dried yeast
¼ cup olive oil
½ cup tomato passata
small handful of basil leaves,
    chopped

1–2 cloves garlic, finely
    chopped
2 large fresh mozzarella balls
    (or 8 bocconcini), sliced
extra-virgin olive oil,
    to drizzle
extra basil leaves, to garnish

Sift the flour and salt into a large bowl and stir in the sugar and yeast. Make a well in the centre and add 200 ml lukewarm water and the oil. Mix to a dough then turn out onto a well-floured surface. Knead for 4–5 minutes, or until smooth. Put the dough in a greased bowl, cover with a tea towel and allow to rise in a warm place for about 1 hour, or until doubled in size.

Preheat the oven to 220°C (Gas 7). Turn the dough out onto a floured surface and divide into 2 equal balls. Roll each ball out until you have 2 thin pizza bases with 25 cm diameters. Carefully transfer to 2 lightly floured baking trays.

Combine the passata, basil and garlic and spread over the bases, leaving 1.5 cm free around the edge. Divide the mozzarella between the bases, drizzle with olive oil and bake for 15–20 minutes, or until the bases are crisp and the cheese has melted. Garnish with basil leaves and serve immediately.

Makes 2 pizzas

Passata is pureed tomatoes! You can buy it in large bottles from supermarkets and delis.

Grandma also has vines of bright red tomatoes.

I can just reach them standing on my tippy toes.

We make margherita pizza with melted mozzarella.

I say, 'Delizioso!' Grandma says, 'Grazie, Bella!'

Beetroot and green bean salad

4 medium beetroot (or 450 g
    can whole baby beets,
    drained and cut in half)
1 tablespoon olive oil
½ cup chopped walnuts or
    pine nuts
300 g green beans, trimmed
    and cut in half

¼ cup finely chopped parsley
2 tablespoons lemon juice
¼ cup extra-virgin olive oil
salt and freshly ground black
    pepper
100 g goat's cheese or ricotta

If using fresh beetroot, preheat the oven to 200°C (Gas 6). Peel the beetroot and cut
each one into 8 pieces. Place in a roasting pan and drizzle with the olive oil. Roast
for 40 minutes, or until the beetroot is tender, turning once or twice. Set aside.

Place the nuts in a small frying pan and toast over low heat for 5 minutes, or
until golden. Cook the beans in a saucepan of boiling water for 3 minutes,
or until tender, then drain. Combine the beans, roasted or canned
beetroot, nuts, parsley, lemon juice and extra-virgin olive oil in a
large bowl and lightly toss. Add salt and pepper to taste.
Divide among 4 plates and crumble
the cheese on top.

Serves 4

If you have caramelised balsamic
vinegar or vino cotto in your pantry,
drizzle a teaspoon over each serving
plate as a finishing touch. Yum!

Next we dig up some beetroots, brush off the soil

And peel them and roast them with olive oil.

They're delicious with green beans and a spoonful of chevre

(Which is how you say goat's cheese if you want to sound clever).

Easy peasy fried rice

1 cup long-grain rice

1 tablespoon vegetable oil

12 green prawns, peeled and deveined

2 rashers free-range bacon, rind removed and diced

1 carrot, grated

1 cup mixed corn and peas (frozen is fine)

2 spring onions, finely sliced

2 eggs, lightly beaten

2 tablespoons soy sauce or tamari

¼ cup coriander leaves

wok

Cook the rice according to the instructions on the packet. Drain and set aside to cool.

Heat the oil in a frying pan or wok over medium heat. Add the prawns and cook, stirring, for 2 minutes, or until lightly golden. Add the bacon and cook for a further 2 minutes. Add the carrot, corn, peas and spring onion and cook for a further 3 minutes. Add the eggs and cook for a further minute, or until set. Add the rice and cook, stirring, for 3–4 minutes. Stir through the soy sauce and coriander and serve immediately.

Serves 4

Alongside the beetroot we grow cobs of corn.

I like it in fried rice with vegies and prawn.

Grandma's recipe is easy – I can cook it myself.

I just need some help reaching Grandma's top shelf.

Chicken herb sandwiches

1 free-range chicken breast

¼ cup mayonnaise

1 tablespoon finely snipped chives or chopped parsley

6 slices wholemeal bread

Place the chicken breast in a small saucepan and cover with water. Bring to the boil then reduce the heat and simmer for 10–12 minutes, or until the chicken has cooked through. Remove from the saucepan and set aside to cool.

When the chicken is cool, shred with your fingers or dice and place in a bowl with the mayonnaise and herbs. Stir until well combined. Place 3 slices of bread on a board, divide the chicken mixture between them and top with another slice of bread. Cut into halves to serve. Alternatively, remove the crusts and cut into 3 pieces for finger sandwiches.

Makes 3 sandwiches

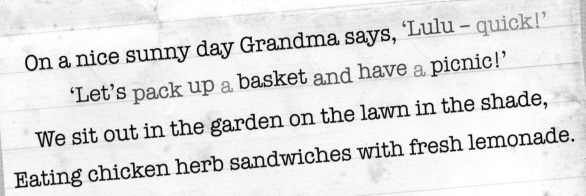

On a nice sunny day Grandma says, 'Lulu – quick!'
'Let's pack up a basket and have a picnic!'
We sit out in the garden on the lawn in the shade,
Eating chicken herb sandwiches with fresh lemonade.

Fresh lemonade

½ cup demerara or raw sugar

⅓ cup lemon juice

mint leaves and ice, to serve

Place the sugar and lemon juice in a saucepan with 5 cups of water. Place over medium heat for 3–4 minutes, stirring occasionally, until the sugar has dissolved. Bring to the boil then lower the heat and simmer for 6–8 minutes. Remove from the heat and refrigerate until chilled. Serve with mint leaves and ice.

Makes 5 cups

Afternoon
Tea

Oatmeal and raisin cookies

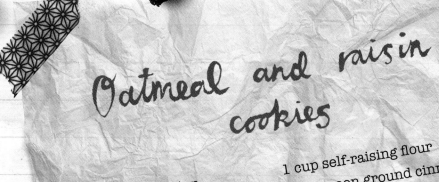

125 g butter
⅔ cup brown sugar
2 tablespoons milk
2 eggs

1 cup self-raising flour
¼ teaspoon ground cinnamon
1½ cups rolled oats
½ cup raisins

By mid-afternoon it's time for a snack
And out of the oven to cool on a rack
Come some cookies we've made with oatmeal and raisins.
Grandma's recipe's so good – they taste just amazing!

Using an electric mixer, cream the butter until soft. Beat in the sugar until light and fluffy. Add the milk and eggs and beat thoroughly. Remove the bowl from the mixer, sift in the flour and cinnamon and lightly stir until just combined. Stir through the oats and raisins. Refrigerate for 2 hours, or until the dough is firm (this is not crucial, but the dough is easier to work with if it's cold).

Preheat the oven to 180°C (Gas 4). Roll heaped tablespoons of dough into balls and arrange 5 cm apart on non-stick or greased baking trays. Press down with a wet fork to flatten slightly.

Bake for about 15 minutes, or until golden. Transfer to a wire rack to cool.

Makes about 28

Apricot and almond slice

125 g butter
⅓ cup caster sugar
2 eggs
2 tablespoons plain flour
1¼ cups ground almonds

pinch of salt
400 g can apricot halves, drained
1 tablespoon apricot jam

Preheat the oven to 180°C (Gas 4). Grease a 22 cm square cake tin with melted butter and line with baking paper.

Using an electric mixer, cream the butter, then beat in the sugar until light and fluffy. Beat in the eggs one at a time. Sift in the flour, add the almond meal and salt and mix until well combined. Spoon into the tin and spread evenly. Place 16 apricot halves on top, cut side up, in a 4 by 4 pattern. Press them lightly into the batter with your fingertips. Bake for 18 minutes, or until a skewer inserted into the centre comes out clean.

While the slice is still hot, heat the jam in a microwave until it is warm and runny, then brush over. Allow the slice to cool in the pan. Cut into 8 pieces (2 apricot halves per piece) and serve.

Serves 8

Next Grandma says, 'Now for apricot slice!'

She lets me do the measuring – I'm very precise!

There are 'teaspoons' and 'cups' and even 'a pinch'.

Once you know what you're doing, it's really a cinch!

Some afternoons I invite a friend over
And with Grandma's help we cook a pavlova.
We beat up the egg whites in Grandma's Sunbeam,
Then we pile the meringue high with berries and cream.

Pavlova

4 egg whites
1 cup caster sugar
1 teaspoon white vinegar
½ teaspoon vanilla extract

300 ml cream, whipped
1 cup sliced strawberries
(or whichever fruit you like)

Preheat the oven to 200°C (Gas 6). (Don't use the fan setting when cooking pavlova.) Place a piece of baking paper onto a baking tray and draw a 20 cm circle with a pencil.

Using an electric mixer, beat the egg whites on high speed until they stand in stiff peaks. Keep beating on high speed and gradually add the sugar 1 tablespoon at a time. Fold in the vinegar and vanilla. Spoon large dollops of the mixture onto the baking paper inside the circle and smooth over the top lightly.

Reduce the oven temperature to 150°C (Gas 2) and bake for 1 hour. If the pavlova browns too quickly, reduce the temperature (but avoid opening the oven door). Turn off the heat and leave the pavlova to cool in the oven with the door slightly ajar. When cool, slide onto a cake plate. Don't worry if the pavlova collapses a little. Spoon over the whipped cream and fruit to serve.

Serves 8-10

Sometimes we pretend we're in a chef's contest.

It helps having Grandma – the judge is impressed!

We make a banana cake and watch as it rises.

The judge thinks it's perfect and gives us all prizes!

Banana cake

125 g butter

¾ cup caster sugar

½ teaspoon vanilla extract

2 eggs

2 large ripe bananas, mashed

½ cup chopped walnuts
   (optional)

1½ cups self-raising flour

¼ teaspoon bicarbonate of soda

⅓ cup milk

Lemon cream cheese icing

60 g cream cheese

25 g butter

1 teaspoon finely grated
   lemon rind

¾ cup icing sugar

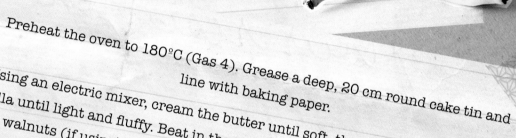

Preheat the oven to 180°C (Gas 4). Grease a deep, 20 cm round cake tin and line with baking paper.

Using an electric mixer, cream the butter until soft, then beat in the sugar and vanilla until light and fluffy. Beat in the eggs, one at a time. Stir through the banana and walnuts (if using), then sift in the flour and gently fold through. Dissolve the bicarbonate of soda in the milk and fold into the mixture. Spoon into the tin, spread evenly and bake for 50 minutes, or until a skewer inserted into the centre comes out clean. Set aside in the tin for 10 minutes before transferring to a wire rack to cool.

To make the icing, beat the cream cheese, butter and rind in an electric mixer until light and fluffy. Gradually beat in the icing sugar. Spread over the top of the cooled cake and serve.

Serves 8

judge

Blueberry muffins

2 cups self-raising flour
¾ cup brown sugar
1 cup buttermilk
¼ cup vegetable oil

1 egg, lightly beaten
2 cups frozen
    blueberries

Grandma also helps me set up my own cafe.

Harry and Teddy are my customers today.

'May I recommend our muffins – they're really delicious!'

They can't pay the bill, but they help wash the dishes.

Preheat the oven to 190°C (Gas 5). Line 12 x ⅓ cup muffin tins with paper cases.

Sift the flour into a large bowl then stir through the sugar. Make a well in the centre and add the buttermilk, oil and egg. Stir until just combined (do not overmix). Gently stir through the blueberries.

Spoon the batter into the paper cases and bake for 25 minutes, or until a skewer inserted into the centres comes out clean. Set aside in the tin for 5 minutes, then transfer to a wire rack to cool. Serve warm or at room temperature.

Makes 12

Sometimes Grandma and I host an afternoon tea.
She has special teacups she saves just for me.
For the whole afternoon we stir and we bake,
But it's definitely worth it for Grandma's cupcakes!

Vanilla cupcakes with passionfruit icing

125 g butter
¾ cup caster sugar
1 teaspoon vanilla extract
2 eggs
2 cups self-raising flour
¾ cup milk

Passionfruit icing
1 cup icing sugar
1½ tablespoons passionfruit pulp

Preheat the oven to 190°C (Gas 5). Line 12 x ⅓ cup muffin tins with cupcake cases.

Using an electric mixer, cream the butter, sugar and vanilla until light and fluffy. Add the eggs one at a time and beat after each addition. Sift the flour and lightly fold half through the mixture, followed by half of the milk. Repeat with the remaining flour and milk. Spoon into the cupcake cases and bake for 15–20 minutes, or until a skewer inserted into the centres comes out clean. Set aside in the tin for 5 minutes, then transfer to a wire rack to cool.

To make the icing, sift the sugar into a bowl and add the passionfruit. Stir until smooth and shiny, adding a little more passionfruit if needed, then spread over the cupcakes (it's fine if the cupcakes are still warm – this will help the icing spread). Set aside until the icing sets, then serve.

Makes 12

We also pretend we've invited the Queen!
I tell Harry, 'She only eats gourmet cuisine!'
When we choose our ingredients we pick only the finest
To make scones and jam for her Royal Highness.

Scores

3 cups self-raising flour
1 teaspoon salt
60 g butter, diced

1¼ cups milk or buttermilk
jam and cream, to serve

Preheat the oven to 230°C (Gas 8). Lightly grease a baking tray.
Sift the flour and salt into a large bowl. Rub in the butter until
the mixture resembles coarse breadcrumbs. Make a well in
the centre and mix in the milk. Pull the dough together into a
rough ball, turn out onto a floured surface and knead lightly.
Pat out to a 2 cm thick round and cut into 5 cm rounds (or
squares if you don't want any waste) with a floured cutter.

Place close together on the baking tray.
Bake for 10–15 minutes, or until well-risen and
golden. Serve warm with jam and cream.

Makes about 10

At dinnertime Grandma writes us a menu
With extravagant dishes – tonight's one is 'ragu'.
But actually it's just a sauce for spaghetti
And, since he's been good, we share it with Teddy.

ragu

grandma's menu

Beef ragu with spaghetti

2 tablespoons olive oil

1 small brown onion, finely chopped

1 carrot, diced

1 celery stalk, diced

1 rasher free-range bacon, rind removed and diced

1 clove garlic, crushed

500 g beef mince

1 cup beef stock

1 cup tomato passata

salt and freshly ground black pepper

375 g spaghetti

grated parmesan cheese, to serve

Heat the oil in a large saucepan over low–medium heat. Add the onion, carrot, celery, bacon and garlic. Cook, stirring, for 6–7 minutes, or until the onion is soft. Increase the heat to medium–high, add the mince and cook, stirring, for a further 3–4 minutes, or until mince begins to brown. Stir in the stock and passata and bring to the boil. Reduce the heat and simmer uncovered, stirring occasionally, for 45 minutes, or until the sauce has reduced to desired consistency. Season with salt and pepper to taste.

Cook the pasta according to the instructions on the packet. Drain and divide between 4 bowls. Spoon over the beef ragu, sprinkle with parmesan cheese and serve.

Serves 4

When I choose what's for dinner I say, 'Pretty please,

'Can we cook my most favourite, macaroni with cheese?'

Grandma grates cheddar cheese for me to fold in,

Then it bakes in the oven until it's golden.

Macaroni cheese

300 g macaroni
½ cup fresh breadcrumbs
½ tablespoon olive oil
40 g butter
¼ cup plain flour
3 cups milk

100 g free-range ham,
    chopped (optional)
1 cup grated gruyere or
    cheddar cheese
1 cup grated parmesan cheese
1 cup frozen peas

Preheat the oven to 190°C (Gas 5). Grease a 2 litre ovenproof baking dish.

Cook the macaroni according to the instructions on the packet. Drain and set aside.

Toss the breadcrumbs in a frying pan over low heat with the olive oil until pale golden, then set aside.

Melt the butter in a saucepan over low–medium heat. Stir in the flour and cook for 1 minute. Add the milk gradually, stirring over low–medium heat until the sauce thickens. Gently mix in the ham (if using), cheeses, peas and macaroni and pour into the baking dish. Scatter with the breadcrumbs and bake for 15–20 minutes, or until golden. Serve immediately.

Serves 4

I like my macaroni with a big green salad on the side!

'Let's be French this evening!' Grandma sometimes will say.
I say, 'Ooh la la!' and put on my beret.
Grandma makes a French quiche for Harry and me.
Would I like seconds? Yes, of course ... I mean 'oui!'

Bacon and onion quiche

1 sheet frozen shortcrust
   pastry, just thawed
1 teaspoon olive oil
1 brown onion, finely chopped
3 rashers free-range bacon,
   rind removed and diced

¾ cup grated gruyere or
   cheddar cheese
3 eggs
1 teaspoon plain flour
pinch of ground nutmeg
300 ml cream
½ cup milk

Preheat the oven to 200°C (Gas 6). Roll out the pastry sheet to fit a 23 cm fluted flan tin (with removable base). Press the pastry gently into the tin, being careful not to stretch it. Trim the edge with a knife so it is level with the top of the tin. Prick the base lightly with a fork. Line the pastry with baking paper and half-fill with dried beans or rice. Bake for 10 minutes, then remove baking paper and beans/rice. Return to the oven for another 5–10 minutes, or until golden brown. Set aside to cool.

Reduce the oven to 180°C (Gas 4). Heat the oil in a small frying pan and cook the onion and bacon over medium heat for 3–4 minutes, or until the onion is soft. Spoon into the pastry case.

Whisk together the cheese, eggs, flour, nutmeg, cream and milk until just combined (overbeating causes bubbles on top). Pour into the pastry case. Bake for about 35 minutes, or until set. Serve warm.

Serves 4–6

When we have guests for dinner we have several courses.

We cook lots of dishes with all different sauces.

Harry wears his best outfit and helps us to serve.

We start with cheese twists – they're called an 'hors d'oeuvre'.

Cheese twists

2 sheets frozen puff pastry
(24 cm x 24 cm), just thawed

1 egg, lightly beaten

½ cup finely grated parmesan
cheese

½ cup finely grated cheddar
cheese

chopping board

Preheat the oven to 200°C (Gas 6). Line a large baking tray with baking paper. Place 1 sheet of pastry on a large chopping board. Brush with the egg and sprinkle evenly with the cheeses. Top with the remaining sheet of pastry and press down firmly. Cut into 2 cm wide strips and twist (there should be 4–5 twists in each strip).

Place the twists on the tray and press the ends down firmly so they do not untwist. Bake for 12 minutes, or until golden brown. Transfer to a wire rack to cool.

Makes 12

Best pumpkin soup

30 g butter
1 brown onion, chopped
2 cloves garlic, chopped
3 rashers free-range bacon,
    rind removed and diced
    (optional)
½ teaspoon ground cumin
½ teaspoon ground nutmeg

1 kg pumpkin, peeled and
    roughly chopped
4 cups chicken stock
¼ cup cream
salt and freshly ground black pepper
2 tablespoons snipped chives, to
    garnish (or you can use parsley
    or coriander leaves)

Melt the butter in a large saucepan over medium heat and cook the onion, garlic and bacon for 3–4 minutes, or until the onion is soft. Add the spices and fry gently for 1 minute. Add the pumpkin and stock. Bring to the boil and simmer, covered, for about 20 minutes, or until the pumpkin is tender.

Cool slightly and puree in several batches in a food processor or blender (or you can use a hand-held stick blender in the saucepan). Return to the saucepan, stir through the cream and gently reheat. Season with salt and pepper to taste. Ladle into serving bowls and garnish with herbs.

Serves 4–6

If you don't have ground cumin or nutmeg in your pantry, don't worry. This soup is still yummy without any spices!

When our guests are all seated we bring out a tray

With our best pumpkin soup to serve for entree.

We eat it with crunchy baguette on the side.

Our friends say it's the best soup that they've ever tried!

Roast chicken with stuffing is the next of our dishes.

With crispy potatoes it's just so delicious.

Grandma lifts up her glass and says, 'Let's make a toast ...

'To Lulu and Harry – for this wonderful roast!'

Roast chicken with lemon herb stuffing

Lemon herb stuffing

1½ cups fresh breadcrumbs
1 celery stalk, finely diced
2 spring onions, finely sliced
¼ cup finely chopped parsley
finely grated rind of 1 lemon
1 egg, lightly beaten
30 g butter, melted

1 x 1.8 kg free-range chicken
20 g butter, melted
6 medium-large potatoes
  (desiree or similar variety)
2 tablespoons olive oil

Preheat the oven to 180°C (Gas 4). Mix the stuffing ingredients in a bowl. Remove the fat from inside the chicken, rinse inside and out with water and pat dry with paper towel. Fill the chicken cavity with stuffing and tie the legs together with kitchen string.

Place the chicken on a rack in a roasting pan. Add enough water to reach 2 cm up the side of the pan (the water should not touch the chicken). Brush the chicken with the butter and roast for 80–90 minutes, basting occasionally, until cooked through (if you pierce the thigh with a skewer, the juices should be clear, not red or pink). If the water evaporates while the chicken is roasting, add a little more.

Meanwhile, peel and quarter the potatoes. Pat dry with paper towel and put in a large roasting pan. Drizzle with the oil and cook for 45 minutes, or until tender and golden brown.

Allow the chicken to rest for 10 minutes, then carve and serve with the stuffing, potatoes and your favourite green vegetable.

Serves 4

Saucy chocolate pudding

1 cup self-raising flour
3 tablespoons cocoa
⅓ cup caster sugar
½ cup milk
100 g butter, melted

2 eggs, lightly beaten
½ teaspoon vanilla extract
¾ cup brown sugar
2 cups boiling water
vanilla ice cream, to serve

Preheat the oven to 180°C (Gas 4). Grease a 1.5 litre souffle dish (which looks a bit like a large ramekin).

Sift the flour and 2 tablespoons of the cocoa into a large bowl. Stir in the caster sugar. Combine the milk, melted butter, egg and vanilla in a jug. Make a well in the dry ingredients and gradually add the milk mixture, lightly stirring until combined (do not overmix). Pour into the baking dish and smooth the top. Evenly sift over the remaining tablespoon of cocoa, then sprinkle with the brown sugar. Gently pour the boiling water on top.

Bake for 35–40 minutes, or until a cake-like top forms and a skewer inserted halfway into the centre comes out clean. Serve hot with vanilla ice cream.

Serves 4–6

ice cream

Then for dessert there's my most favourite thing –
Vanilla ice cream and chocolate pudding!
We lick every last bit from our plates and our spoons.
As our guests leave they say, 'Please invite us back soon!'

It's the best fun there is being Grandma's sous-chef

And we're such good eaters there's never much left.

I want to grow up to be just like Grandma

And be the best ever cook in the whole world by far!

Equipment

baking dish

blender

baking tray

cake tins

chopping board

electric mixer

flan tin

frying pan

grater

food processor

jug

measuring cups

1 cup = 250 ml

measuring spoons

1 teaspoon = 5 ml

muffin tin

ramekins

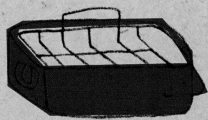

roasting pan

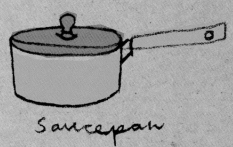

saucepan

sieve

skewers

spatula

whisk

wok

Acknowledgements

To my darling Grandma, Margaret, the inspiration for this book. Thank you for sharing your passion for good food with me. You have shaped all of our lives in the most extraordinary way.

To my wonderful husband, John, whose support is boundless. You mean the world to me.

To my sister, Kate, who shared Grandma's kitchen with me. A little girl's greatest gift is surely a big sister, and none is better than mine.

To my Mum, Suzanne, one of this country's finest and most knowledgeable food writers. Thank you for always putting your family first. We would all be lost without you.

To my Dad, Robert – an accomplished cook in his own right – thank you for your never-ending kindness and generosity. Your unwavering belief in me has meant more than you can imagine.

Extra special thanks to the very clever Michelle Mackintosh. Your superb illustrations and design have exceeded all my expectations. You have brought Grandma, Lulu and Harry to life just perfectly.

Finally, a huge thank you to all the team at Hardie Grant for this wonderful opportunity. Thanks to Helen Chamberlin for your fine editing. And particular thanks to my Publisher, Paul McNally, and Editor, Jane Winning, for your enthusiasm, patience and sound advice – we made it!

Published in 2011 by Hardie Grant Books

Hardie Grant Books (Australia)
85 High Street
Prahran, Victoria 3181
www.hardiegrant.com.au

Hardie Grant Books (UK)
Second Floor, North Suite
Dudley House
Southampton Street
London WC2E 7HF
www.hardiegrant.co.uk

Cataloguing-in-Publication data is available from the
National Library of Australia.
My Grandma's Kitchen
ISBN: 978 1 74270 114 1

Designed and illustrated by Michelle Mackintosh
Edited by Helen Chamberlin
Colour reproduction by Splitting Image Colour Studio
Printed and bound in China by C&C Offset Printing

The publisher would like to thank nordliving for supplying the beautiful
props that appear in this book.